Ma nt i s

Ma nt i s

David Dowker

chax 2018

ISBN 978-1-946104-10-6

Chax Press / PO Box 162 / Victoria, TX 77902-0162

Library of Congress Cataloging-in-Publication Data

Names: Dowker, David, 1955- author.
Title: Mantis / David Dowker.
Description: Victoria, TX : Chax Press, 2018.
Identifiers: LCCN 2018001949 | ISBN 9781946104106 (alk. paper)
Classification: LCC PR9199.4.D6874 M36 2018 | DDC 811/.6--dc23
LC record available at https://lccn.loc.gov/2018001949

Chax Press is supported in part by the School of Arts &
Sciences at the University of Houston-Victoria. We are located
in the UHV Center for the Arts in downtown Victoria, Texas.
We acknowledge the support of graduate and undergraduate
student interns, and press assistants who contribute to the books
we publish. In 2018 our interns are Renee Raven, Claudia De Luna,
Ben Leitner, and Ann Cefola, and our student asssistant is Jennifer
Hernandez. The book is also supported by private donors.
We are thankful to all of our contributors and members.

Please see *http://chax.org/support/* for more information.

Ma nt i s

"root notes of a transient present"

(Clark Coolidge – *The Maintains*)

1   such

        ratio
instrumental   like

        to whom

                                        spring

                                        2

        the near   as   for

                knot

                                                        the   true scales
that fair

        part   of those

                                        note
come to   one

id   at which

     in full

          flower   a   gate

of another   or the like

     tremor

                                    a mote

                                         hence

any of several

     natural

forms meaning

     leaves

3
                                    sending forth

or more

                                              phase

                                                   nodules

                                    and rind

                                         of

the arboreal   the
                                                     loose or
                                                 has been like

4

lobed

                                                 past

                                                 blister   as sap
                                                 due from

                                                 cynosure

state   being   5

                                                 canopic

often

          cast off   wound
                                                       coupon
shuns   in reply to

6

the one   that   hums

            huddles
    near
        cathode

        hollow

subject
            to

        diurnal   en
during

7

                                any

                        program

                        given

                        ordinal   table

                        outline against

                                            shine

                        as thrown on   paper

8

shift
    trope

point
  dense

with
  similar

breadth

nascent

clear
                                  doubt

enter into

having

9

          gloss   dark
       region of   wheat

         motion without

    figurative

           flows
  innate

attributive
               principle

10

        inhabit   carbon

root   present

                                  telling the whole

effects of

                                      valence

11

                         thing

                             beam

       the

                           abound

        usual   plural
that which

                        expend
                        against
                        conveyance

having only

        past

object   extension   embodied

vitreous
        growth
           rate
     part
the first   word   as
                                    compound
  bred by   orifice or
          shape
               solvent   in   like stance
                 of this   such as   arose
                                    below

12

as of
              ~~shadow~~
                from umbra

ingot
not   rhodochrosite
     being

13   pertain   to   pitch
                                                      mineral

so   to render
allegiance
one who
              thought to be
                                                                            pith

              of which we
                                                      so thus

        in   air
terrestrial
                                                      14

                                                          arrow
                                                                    s

                                                                          osmosis

                                                              cell

                  or gland   matrices
interior   matter   as often

                                                          ops

                                                          outside

notes   delimit

field

                    or flense

           scape

gibbous

    sentence

      hence

semifluid

  zen

             automatic

  curve

apparatus

           consonant

15

           aspirate

coherence   sequence

deeply

                    flumes

                                                cave in

16

                    all

resin   a state
     fled   greater than any
                                                          of this
that which is

          meaning   17
          yields

                                          come   to
                                                          loosely

having   body   through
     spark

                                               multiple

out of

                                          woof

song
made

to remove
   what   supports   changeable
a set   measure
as the   harsher   possibly
        particular

dipoles

   light hammers
  higher

18

geological
click

                                    pupa

                      machine
       perpendicular   prompt

                     warp

     the like

19

once held   spectacle

                                      star
                                 perpetual

                as   control
                             optical

   god
        object   21
having no   part of the
pinnate   in
        a given period   sum of

     another   collective
   mobile
mind   fine-tooth
bower   filter

                            comb   through
20
                                brain
            ark   capital

twine

conglomerate

luminous
wasp

bot
set

such

light
in   plum
or the like

state

distillate

23

22   swoon

factor

octave
probe
wave   to deter

gymnasia

adherent

24

rapt

reflex   apex

concurrence   optic
    cone

pan

    nucleic

                                            just
                                            earth
                                            having

orb

floats in air   sun

    glyphs   setting

jurassic

                                    even

as

only

blot
out or

in as much
and

25

ordinate
azurite

on

similar   to
being

26

calyx

otherwise

nothing   means

pitch brings

rise in
spoke

mere

cesium
poll

coterie

orchid

register

which   ravels

shorn
jargon

                                                    state
        rush

                                        speech
                    cannot

        quartz

        spore

                                carbonate   gloss
                    any
                        who wane

            under
hypothetics

                        bling
27   surge

grace   overt

                    28

                        elsewhere

either

    syllabic
                        here
              versed

              bent   line

whorl
      or gone
    to ground
              done
said
    goad

                rather

check   polar

29   30

valence   haploid

case

32

drawn by

drub

lobate   path

radiolarian   code time

31

block   verb

depth
agent

cut clear   33
          mirror

radical

made   address
active

nucleus

35

ionic

ratio

this   which

erasure

36

verbals   peregrine

34

actinic
spring
or the like

infinitive

voltaic
aphid

as   hinge

rocks

insert

37

locust

zeolite

locus   sleep

38

render

eye

shunt   any

dim

another   fit

rare

scale

part   clack

to part

as   cleft

gave   one of   gull or

flavor

gorm

39

40

sound

akin to

partition

                    alkali

              lacquer   plasm
                                                echelon

yields   bivalent
          wicker

sired
                                                                being

among other
troth

mantid   the after
          being   hence

41

aqueous

arbutus   prime
        gloom

                                         43

42

                                             matrix server   or
    indwell   spore

        to be   terminal

                                     daub   globose
    and cease
        only in

crease

                                                        pelagic
genus

                                         44

        as   flush
                                 loose

tone

                    slag   bulk
consonant

                                            45

                                      put that

                                                    as   in
                                                          part or   like

            but not

                                      archaeopteryx   means

                                                          twig

                                                          fig
annealed   ear   in
                                      form

                                                                or evince

                    latch

                                            46

                                      bring

                                                    done

        at   an one
it   as coils   gerund

```
                                              47
            cap
                                                    pop be
        none                                  peony
                                              pen   to

pronoun
                                              concrete      now

velocity
chops
                        bop                   freed
phenol
                                              reflex    flux pulse
          mute

   flat
                                              eye

           must                               calyx

stops
     spot                                     48

              to that                         one's lot


            predicate
```

hydrogen   warble

49

having   color

living

                    iamb
                    prismic

        baffle

certain   verb   felt

                                    control
basalt   mirror   warp

                        earth   terms

below

50

onyx   twill

    silicate

    full   of

                                    gog

dwell

  well   hazard   come
                                 due
                           anyplace

51

lambent   52

whack   parallel
                           opera

  so

motile
            bolden   sung

em
bud   54

                                              squilla
53

cell   cotangent

                                              infra-
                                              local

                                                        inter-
          text   opt

cipher   set

hue

hob

bottom

full
hull

hither

55
bodily

grivet
56

nascence

grim as
got

privity
abates
risen still

ilk

scale

as stasis

sum   58

                              fume   time
            thrum
                                       beyond

57   rhomb
                                                          iris
            diatom

        box

spikenard   statics

                                              arc
    derive   cast
                                  within

        alike

59

which   at

        put
                that   tensor
                                                over

                                                60

                                                nomad
                                                                        as space

                pleistocene
        behind us
                                                index

                                                having
        as last

adjective

61   whorl

oxide
word   62

                                                     note
                                                     bolt
                                                             tilt

    order   order

                                                     convex

                                                                      state

                word   much

                                                     as above

phrases
slip

burlap
cup

63   O

made

more
widely   chimera
by
some   dim   other
                                    64

anew   noise

base

ever

pitch

rose

        through citron

                                             stitch
                                             blip

65   66

        nautilus   nodular

       also
     apt

                                             block   that

gap   concave
pith
                                          hone
           with   hence
              lapwing   mute

yield

puma

precede

67   uranium

anode

numeral

unit

gem   68

word
lobe
tenable   doctrine   letter
                           choice
web mode   becomes one
                                     dispersal

ester

let

utter

                                    traduce

                                    cubics
hobble   by

                stalagmite

        or
      runic
            spring
                                        inner
                                                    din
69
                                        concrete
            tumult   acumen

                nebula
                                        given
  allow
  hydrous   ablative

70

mode

postulate

protozoa   any
                                               like verb
                                         become
vessel   glacial   opal

interval
                                         71

cell   display   zarf
emit   part
        its
                                            highly
                                         roentgen

                                                 per
light   charge

                                         folds to
                                         quell
        triturate   being

                                         module

72

any one of

antiphonal

toxin

among   reverb

block

usage   figure

meaning

spoken   else

abate

arrow   code

breeds

agate

73

corollary   74

blip

pod   imp

osis

tourmaline

dwindle

that

panicle

75

blast   plait   plain
  with   refusal
part   <u>period</u>
  of   to
certain   lease

brain
cite

76

      plexus
        rescinded

zygote

     pitch

merge

      to err
spindly

bit

     tremor

    ovate

       pulmonate

77

      fault
being
         oneness

       factor

     attributes

         as
           grammar

relative to

twining

after
     risen

like
to

means usual

lag

nucleus

78
all these

derived   sense

platonic

numbers

79

limit   subtle
means

to
the been

leastwise

bound
against

death

mass   mind
as   surly   during

porous   ore
                                    foil
                                       to foil
folded

these mineral
                states
          by way of

80   flow

     erasure
     basis   81

                                    at loss

                                         cause

     principally

                          deepens
                          as   measure

squares   83

                                     loopdom

something   outlying
                                     purl
                                                    circuit

            like frame
         incorporated

82

      alternate

                  carrier

a tell
shell
partiality   molar
         bridge

splint

lodestar

84   audible

prolepsis

given leave   thickening

to leave   speed
dactyls   86

iscariot of   chirp
elvis

keep
85
drawn
heliocentric

as from

leaven

plinth

dial   hydride   within   time

87

      by like   coition

            fold

seal

          found

                  fault

consonant   outlet

            89

    dipole

           rises

88

oosphere

over

      other   cog

                                          core

circular   set
        pending
          ray

plural

                                        algebraic
                                        pitch

                                      montage
remunerative   phosphorous

90   flowers

tonic

91

aster
polymer

enough   to be

  bound

92

   the hum

        also

     shines

friction
     which

93

              implies

by

light

                   stop

                 parts
               that

                noun

                  own

94

stone   period
as   would come

    to
      this

zinc

arc

95

due
to   dash as
    lastly

stirs

96

the much

which   even
about such
so   said

as yet

    having   means

   glean

97

then again

98

shine

as rose   and then   to flow
through   clear

                    to   cross that
such that

yet again

                tense
    hence   as if

about the author

David Dowker was born in Kingston, Ontario but has lived most of his life in Toronto. He was editor of *The Alterran Poetry Assemblage* from 1996 to 2004 (which can be accessed at Library and Archives Canada). He published *Machine Language* in 2010, and *Virtualis: Topologies of the Unreal* (with Christine Stewart) in 2013 (shortlisted for the Stephan G. Stephansson Award for poetry).

about chax

Founded in 1984 in Tucson, Arizona, Chax has published 200 books in a variety of formats, including hand printed letterpress books and chapbooks, hybrid chapbooks, book arts editions, and trade paperback editions such as the book you are holding. In August 2014 Chax moved to Victoria, Texas, and is presently located in the University of Houston-Victoria Center for the Arts, which has generously supported the publication of *At Night on the Sun*, which has also received support from many friends of the press. Chax is an independent 501(c)(3) organization which depends on support from various government and private funders, and, primarily, from individual donors and readers.

Recent and books include *The Complete Light Poems*, by Jackson Mac Low, *Life–list*, by Jessica Smith, *Andalusia*, by Susan Thackrey, *Diesel Hand*, by Nico Vassilakis, *Dark Ladies*, by Steve McCaffery, *What We Do*, by Michael Gottlieb, *Limerence*, by Saba Razvi, *Short Course*, by Ted Greenwald and Charles Bernstein, *An Intermittent Music*, by Ted Pearson, *Arrive on Wave*, by Gil Ott, *Entangled Bank*, by James Sherry, *Auto-cinema*, by Gaspar Orozco, *The Letters of Carla, the letter b.*, by Benjamin Hollander, *A Mere Ica*, by Linh Dinh, *Visible Instruments*, by Michael Kelleher, *Diesel Hand* (letterpress), by Nico Vassilakis, and *At Night on the Sun*, by Will Alexander, *Title*, by Serge Gavronsky, and *The Hindrances of Householders*, by Jennifer Bartlett.

You may find CHAX online at *https://chax.org*